11+ Vocabulary

For students who want to excel in the 11+ exams and beyond

Download free worksheets & educational resources at www.thetutoress.com/resources

Passage 1

Each year, more than one million people immigrate to the United States in the hope of starting their lives *afresh*. One symbol of mass migration is the Statue of Liberty; a figure that has become an emblem of American life. The Statue of Liberty is located on Liberty Island in Manhattan. At 151 feet, the Statue is the tallest and most recognisable monument in America. The monument stands on a pedestal which was actually financed by the American people themselves. However, the Statue itself was in fact a gift from the French. Some might therefore argue that it is an insignia of collaboration, representing two countries and two vastly different cultures coming together to produce something magnificent and undeniably striking.

Section I: *From the passage*

Select the best synonym to replace the word/phrase in the sentence.

1   Each year more than one million people **immigrate** to the United States in the hopes of starting their lives afresh.

    (a) leave   (b) move   (c) devour   (d) assist

2   One symbol of mass migration is the Statue of Liberty; a figure that has become an **emblem** of American life.

    (a) contraption (b) pedestal   (c) representation (d) vessel

3   At 151 feet, the Statue is the tallest and most **recognisable** monument in America.

    (a) hidden   (b) covert   (c) obscure   (d) apparent

4   The Statue stands on a pedestal which was actually **financed** by the American people themselves.

    (a) rebuffed   (b) backed   (c) ratified   (d) spurned

5   Some might therefore argue that it is an **insignia** of collaboration, representing two countries and two vastly different cultures coming together to produce something magnificent and undeniably striking.

    (a) adumbration (b) receptacle (c) hallmark   (d) opening

Section II: More from the passage

Match each word on the left with its synonym on the right. The first has been done for you.

(1)	afresh	:	f	(a)	partnership
(2)	located	:	____	(b)	prominent
(3)	pedestal	:	____	(c)	situated
(4)	in fact	:	____	(d)	dispute
(5)	argue	:	____	(e)	indisputably
(6)	collaboration	:	____	(f)	~~anew~~
(7)	vastly	:	____	(g)	glorious
(8)	different	:	____	(h)	greatly
(9)	magnificent	:	____	(i)	actually
(10)	undeniably	:	____	(j)	diverse
(11)	striking	:	____	(k)	dais

Section III: Vocabulary Booster

Choose the most suitable answer to replace the vocabulary in the sentence. Remember to take into account if the word you have chosen will fit in the context of the sentence.

1   He was in no position to **oppose** his father's decision that he would take over the family's business upon graduation, because he had been brought up to obey his parents' wishes.

    (a) accept   (b) insist   (c) disagree   (d) resist

2   In his bid to **contest** the evidence given by the prosecutor's witness, the defendant's lawyer called in an expert witness to evaluate the witness' statement.

    (a) struggle   (b) dispute   (c) compete   (d) advocate

3   Stringent security checks are carried out at airports to ensure that no passengers carry **concealed** weapons or items of potential danger to aircrafts and passengers.

    (a) hidden   (b) displayed   (c) covert   (d) obscured

4   The police kicked on the door expecting to catch the criminal red-handed; however the door flew open to **reveal** an old man in his pajamas, standing at the doorway of his kitchen with a mug of tea in his hands and a look of bewilderment on his face.

    (a) divulge   (b) cover   (c) hide   (d) show

5   The factory has been outfitted with state-of-the-art machinery and is ready to **commence** operations next week.

    (a) end   (b) begin   (c) work   (d) cease

6   As the firemen had protective masks on, they did not have to suffer the **acrid** fumes from the burning chemical plant.

    (a) intense   (b) savoury   (c) unpleasant (d) pungent

7   The patrons of the bar breathed a sigh of relief when the manager removed the **boorish** drunk who had been traumatising the waitresses and annoying the other patrons despite repeated warnings.

    (a) unattractive (b) churlish   (c) mannerly   (d) unkind

8   My father holds a certain disdain for politicians and is very **cynical** of anyone who promises to introduce sweeping reforms once they are voted into office.

(a) distrusting (b) optimistic   (c) trusting   (d) supportive

9   Just because the new teacher scorned the dated education practices and had new ideas about teaching strategies that differed from the peers, her views were considered **heresy** and she was even ostracised by her peers.

(a) orthodoxy (b) fallacy   (c) blasphemy (d) dissent

10   In the aftermath of a recent spike in domestic violence, the MP's speech about the necessity of having policies in place to protect victims of such atrocities was **poignant** and left the audience rather sad, but thoughtful.

(a) unemotional (b) sentimental (c) unaffected (d) moving

Passage 2

Nelson Mandela is widely regarded as being one of the world's most illustrious figures because of his determination to end the racist apartheid regime of South Africa. He believed that society should treat all people regardless of their ethnic, cultural or religious background equally. Despite being imprisoned for twenty-seven years, he defied belief by becoming South Africa's first black president in 1990. He was commemorated for his achievements and was awarded the Nobel Peace Prize in 1993. His story has inspired millions of people to fight for equality, treat others with respect and stand up in the face of injustice.

Section I: *From the passage*

Select the best synonym to replace the word in the sentence.

1   Nelson Mandela is widely regarded as being one of the world's most
    illustrious figures because of his determination to end the racist
    apartheid regime of South Africa.

    (a) regular   (b) esteemed   (c) unknown   (d) insignificant

2   He believed that society should treat all people regardless of their ethnic,
    cultural or religious background ***equally***.

    (a) appropriately (b) justly   (c) proportionately (d) unfairly

3   Despite being imprisoned for twenty-seven years, he ***defied*** belief by
    becoming South Africa's first black president in 1990.

    (a) mocked   (b) challenged   (c) encouraged   (d) complimented

4   He was ***commemorated*** for his achievements and was awarded the
    Nobel Peace Prize in 1993.

    (a) memorialised   (b) denounced   (c) overlooked   (d) monument

5   His story has ***inspired*** millions of people to fight for equality, treat others
    with respect and stand up in the face of injustice.

    (a) dissuaded (b) discouraged (c) emboldened   (d) spurned

Section II: More from the Passage -- Opposites Attract

Match each word on the left with its most appropriate antonym on the right. The first has been done for you.

(1)	widely	: d	(a)	equality
(2)	most	: _____	(b)	criticism
(3)	end	: _____	(c)	truce
(4)	believed	: _____	(d)	~~narrowly~~
(5)	achievement	: _____	(e)	disregarded
(6)	imprisoned	: _____	(f)	begin
(7)	first	: _____	(g)	failures
(8)	awarded	: _____	(h)	least
(9)	fight	: _____	(i)	refused
(10)	respect	: _____	(j)	last
(11)	injustice	: _____	(k)	liberated

Section III: Vocabulary Booster

Fill in the blanks below with the following words to complete the passage.

visage	single-handedly	treasure	irk	resolved
ascending	undertake	determined	escaped	resolved

Meanwhile the Captain of the thieves having (1) _____ with his life, (2) _____ to the forest in hot wrath and sore (3) _____ of mind; and his senses were scattered and the colour of his (4) _____ vanished like (5) _____ smoke. Then he thought the matter over again and again, and at last he firmly (6) _____ that he should take the life of Ali, else he would lose all the (7) _____ which his enemy, by knowledge of the magical words, would take away and turn to his own use. Furthermore, he was (8) _____ that he would (9) _____ the business (10) _____.

Section IV: Synonyms Booster

Select one word that has the closest meaning to the word on the left.

1	**Depreciate**	Choose	Apex	Select	Decrease	Zenith
2	**Churlish**	Truculent	Angelic	Diplomatic	Stubborn	Independent
3	**Poignant**	Rotund	Polished	Exhausted	Happy	Sad
4	**Enthusiasm**	Apex	Wisdom	Insincerity	Politeness	Alacrity
5	**Compassion**	Animosity	Malice	Pity	Gall	Sickness

Passage 3

Tigers are widely considered to be one of the most fierce and powerful animals on earth. However, despite their supposed strength, they are in fact one of the world's most vulnerable creatures and face a high risk of extinction. Statistics show that at the beginning of the 20th century, there were more than 100,000 tigers living in the wild. However, by the end of the 20th century, that number had dwindled to approximately 3,000. The greatest threat to the existence of tigers is homo sapiens. Tigers are hunted, stripped of their skin and killed for their body parts. In some parts of the world, the body parts of tigers are a much-desired commodity because they are believed to contain healing properties.

Section I: *From the passage*

Select the best synonym to replace the word in the sentence.

1 Despite their supposed strength, tigers are in fact one of the world's most **vulnerable** creatures and face a high risk of extinction.

   (a) protected   (b) guarded   (c) unsusceptible (d) defenceless

2 **Statistics** show that at the beginning of the 20th century, there were more than 100,000 tigers living in the wild.

   (a) fabrication   (b) concept   (c) data   (d) experience

3 However, by the end of the 20th century, that number had **dwindled** to approximately 3,000.

   (a) increased   (b) declined   (c) decayed   (d) prolonged

4 Tigers are hunted, **stripped** of their skin and killed for their body parts.

   (a) divested   (b) diverted   (c) deprived   (d) disrobed

5 In some parts of the world, the body parts of tigers are a much-desired **commodity** because they are believed to contain healing properties.

   (a) product   (b) produce   (c) phenomenon (d) gizmo

Section II: *More from the passage*

Complete the following crossword puzzle to gain a better understanding of the vocabulary in the passage.

Another word for...

Across

4	the state of being	:	_____
6	curing, to make healthy	:	_____
7	pursued and captured	:	_____
8	deemed to be	:	_____
9	hazard, danger	:	_____

Down

1	close to, roughly	:	_____
2	wild, savage, hostile	:	_____
3	physically strong	:	_____
4	dying out, coming to an end	:	_____
5	peril, trouble	:	_____

Section III: Vocabulary Booster

Fill in the blanks below with the following words to complete the passage.

helpful	items	dense	tendency	impulse
potentially	extremely	apparently	purchasing	advantageous

Shopping for food can be (1) _____ enjoyable. However, before (2) _____ anything it's (3) _____ to know what you want to buy. One way of doing this is to write a shopping list which contains all of the (4) _____ you want to buy. Shopping lists are (5) _____ as they can (6) _____ save you time and money. Some people believe that one should never shop on an empty stomach. (7) _____, research findings show that when shoppers are hungry when they shop for food, they have a (8) _____ to act on (9) _____ and purchase more calorically (10) _____ food.

Passage 4

Did you know that on average, we spend approximately one third of our lives (25 years) sleeping? However, most of us can barely recollect what we experience during our sleep. During sleep, our bodies commence a sophisticated cycle of renewal that is imperative in reestablishing our health and well-being. Sleep is divided into two stages: stages one and two. During stage one we begin to drift off and our bodies will involuntarily jerk. Scientists refer to this jerking motion as a hypnic jerk. In the second stage of sleep, our body temperatures drop and our hearts begin to slow down. This is followed by deep sleep where our tissues regrow and our immune system is revivified.

Section I: *From the passage*

Select the best synonym to replace the word in the sentence.

1   However, most of us can barely **recollect** what we experience during our sleep.

    (a) contrive   (b) lose   (c) summon   (d) remember

2   During sleep, our bodies commence a sophisticated cycle of renewal that is **imperative** in reestablishing our health and well-being.

    (a) critical   (b) discretionary (c) inessential (d) pressing

3   During stage one we begin to drift off and our bodies will **involuntarily** jerk.

    (a) cautiously (b) uncontrollably (c) unenthusiastically (d) warily

4   Scientists refer to this jerking motion as a hypnic **jerk**.

    (a) twitch   (b) jolt   (c) wriggle   (d) shiver

5   This is followed by deep sleep where our tissues regrow and our immune system is **revivified**.

    (a) enervated   (b) gladdened   (c) comforted   (d) rejuvenated

Section II: *More from the passage*

Complete the following word search activity to gain a better understanding of the vocabulary in the passage.

Begin by answering the questions with a word that can be found in the passage. Next, search for the word you have identified in the puzzle.

While you were sleeping...

```
W  N  B  Q  E  S  M  X  L  A  W  E  N  E  R
G  I  D  D  R  O  R  K  Q  L  R  Q  X  I  I
L  M  F  I  T  P  D  V  O  J  R  P  H  Y  U
P  M  H  I  V  H  D  A  T  U  E  E  Z  F  K
D  U  O  D  E  I  N  C  F  R  Q  Q  L  K  R
V  N  G  G  T  S  D  C  I  I  Q  X  A  N  L
L  E  R  E  T  T  A  E  R  O  C  P  O  P  F
X  E  H  A  N  I  N  V  D  A  K  T  Y  O  K
C  E  G  J  S  C  B  C  L  X  B  P  T  S  U
D  E  D  U  E  A  A  H  J  G  N  O  N  D  B
S  J  Y  S  R  T  C  G  N  R  M  M  A  Y  P
S  X  M  E  P  E  G  A  R  E  V  A  F  G  K
E  U  L  Y  L  D  E  P  A  N  W  W  R  T  B
S  Y  V  L  Y  Q  P  N  Q  Z  S  H  M  N  C
C  F  U  Y  T  T  C  X  S  S  B  M  S  V  P
```

Identify a word or a phrase in the passage that has the same meaning as the following words. The first letter is provided for you.

1   regeneration   :   r_____

2   almost not; scarcely   :   b_____

3   intricate   :   s_____

4   split   :   d_____

5   phases   :   s_____

6   fall asleep   :   d_____ off

7   a typical amount   :   a_____

8   resistant   :   i_____

9   encounter   :   e_____

10   movement   :   m_____

Section III: Vocabulary Booster

Fill in the blanks below with the following words to complete the passage.

centered	maintained	practised	decay	preserving
subsequently	famed	deliberately	vast	thus

The ancient Egyptian civilization is (1) _____ for its (2) _____ pyramids which are more than five thousand years old. Daily life in ancient Egypt was heavily (3) _____ around religious worship and (4) _____, there were many temples. Ancient Egyptians (5) _____ a strong belief in the afterlife and (6) _____ built pyramids as tombs for the pharaohs.

The ancient Egyptians also (7) _____ mummification – the art of (8) _____ a body, either human or animal. The Egyptian mummies were made by (9) _____ drying the body. By eliminating moisture, the source of (10) _____ is removed. They dried the body by using a salt mixture called natron.

Section IV: Synonyms Booster

Select one word that has the closest meaning to the word on the left.

1	**Resolute**	Freedom	Admire	Determined	Evolve	Answer
2	**Diminish**	Decrease	View	Orbit	Resolve	Discover
3	**Revolve**	Enlighten	Polish	Stand	Orbit	Stumble
4	**Alleviate**	Intensify	Identify	Hold	Hamper	Relieve
5	**Exasperate**	Condemn	Enrage	Falsify	Coat	Approve

Passage 5

The Greeks believed that the home of their omnipotent deity, Zeus, was on the top of Mount Olympus – a high and lofty mountain whose summit, wrapt in clouds and mist, was hidden from mortal view. Here youth never ages, and the passing years leave no traces on its favoured inhabitants. On the cloud-capped summit of Olympus was the palace of Zeus and Hera, of burnished gold, chased silver, and gleaming ivory. Lower down were the homes of the other gods, which, though less commanding in position and size, were similar to that of Zeus' in design and workmanship. Below these were other palaces of silver, ebony, ivory, or burnished brass, where the Demi-gods, resided.

Section I: *From the passage*

Select the best synonym to replace the word in the sentence.

1   The Greeks believed that the home of their **omnipotent** deity, Zeus, was on the top of Mount Olympus.

    (a) impotent   (b) important   (c) colossal   (d) almighty

2   Mount Olympus was a high and lofty mountain whose summit, wrapt in clouds and mist, was hidden from **mortal** view.

    (a) fatal   (b) human   (c) implacable   (d) tangible

3   Here youth never ages, and the passing years leave no traces on its **favoured** inhabitants.

    (a) privileged   (b) unpopular   (c) prejudiced   (d) exempted

4   Lower down were the homes of the other gods, which, though less **commanding** in position and size, were similar to that of Zeus' in design and workmanship.

    (a) compelling   (b) decisive   (c) unassertive   (d) dominating

5   Below these were other palaces of silver, ebony, ivory, or burnished brass, where the Demi-gods, **resided**.

    (a) dwelled   (b) endured   (c) permeated   (d) bunked

Section II: *More from the passage*

Fill in the blanks with the following words to complete the sentences and to gain a better understanding of the vocabulary featured in the passage.

summit	lofty	youth	inhabitants	workmanship
similar	hidden	passing	burnished	deity

1   Let's meet at the _____ at 3:30 p.m. so we can ski the last run down the mountain together.

2   "Any explanation that relies on something supernatural, such as a _____, is not science!" he declared firmly, trying to douse the superstitious beliefs of his aged mother.

3   It is hard to believe that our strait-laced friend was a passionate political activist in his _____.

4   There are no rivers or lakes on the islands of Bermuda, so the _____ must use rain for water.

5   The struggles of life had taken a toll on her – each _____ year brought new struggles, new obstacles and a couple of lines to her weather-beaten face.

6   Most warranties cover repair or replacement of defective elements due to faulty _____ or materials and are usually in effect for a period of time.

7   The island is mountainous in the main, with a number of _____ upland plains in the east, and volcanic in the west.

8   She had taken extra care in her appearance today and her usually wild and unruly hair gleamed like _____ copper.

9   She felt the loss already, a pain _____ to the loss of her beloved mother so many years ago.

10   He had kept his identity _____ for five years now, but he knew deep down that it couldn't last forever and dreaded the day when he would have to reveal his true identity to those he had come to love and respect.

Section III: Vocabulary Booster
Fill in the blanks below with the following words to complete the passage.

casual	whites	job	folded	wedding
formal	laundry	tie	occasions	suit

Different clothes are required for different (1) _____. For (2) _____ occasions such as a (3) _____ interview or a friend's (4) _____, men might wear a formal (5) _____ and a (6) _____. For informal occasions such as a backyard barbeque, they will probably wear something (7) _____, such as a pair of jeans and a T-shirt.

When your clothes get dirty, it's time to do the (8) _____. Usually clothes are separated into the (9) _____ and the colours. After the clothes are washed and dried, they are ironed or (10) _____ and put away.

Passage 6

They travelled on without speech, saving their breath for the work of their bodies. On every side was silence, pressing upon them with a tangible presence. It affected their minds as the many atmospheres of deep water affect the body of the diver. It crushed them with the weight of unending vastness and unalterable decree. It crushed them into the remotest recesses of their own minds, pressing out of them, like juices from the grape, all the false ardours and exaltations and undue self-values of the human soul, until they perceived themselves finite and small, specks and motes, moving with weak cunning and little wisdom amidst the play and inter-play of the great blind elements and forces.

Section I: *From the passage*

Select the best synonym to replace the word in the sentence.

1   On every side was silence, pressing upon them with a **tangible** presence.

    (a) imperceptible (b) abstract (c) sensible (d) palpable

2   It crushed them with the weight of unending vastness and **unalterable** decree.

    (a) inflexible (b) required (c) unchangeable (d) unbroken

3   It **crushed** them into the remotest recesses of their own minds…

    (a) trampled (b) embraced (c) crowded (d) surrendered

4   …pressing out of them, like juices from the grape, all the false **ardours** and exaltations and undue self-values of the human soul…

    (a) apathy (b) lethargy (c) pretentions (d) zeal

5   …until they perceived themselves **finite** and small, specks and motes, moving with weak cunning and little wisdom amidst the play and inter-play of the great blind elements and forces.

    (a) endless (b) limited (c) exact (d) unfixed

Section II: *More from the passage*

Fill in the blanks with the following words to complete the sentences and to gain a better understanding of the vocabulary featured in the passage.

remotest	exaltation	atmosphere	perceived	presence
decree	vastness	undue	speech	speck

1 The _____ of the region has always given its people an independent, frontiersman spirit.

2 The doctor said that he would be able to go home in ten days, provided he wasn't subjected to any _____ stress.

3 She heaved with painful sobs, rendering _____ impossible.

4 By the time they made it to the cafeteria, three hours after the designated lunch hour, not a _____ of food was in sight.

5 She had not seen him for so long that his _____ was the best part of her birthday party.

6 Of existing species the bear, wild-boar, badger and roe-deer may occasionally be seen in the _____ wilds of mountain and forest.

7 Being ever the most consummate host, she firmly believed that having live music could really add to the celebratory _____ as guests relax and enjoy themselves.

8 She beamed with _____ at the thought of finally being able to marry the love of her life.

9 It is a marketing fact that mediocre products are _____ to be more valuable if they are overpriced.

10 After the hurricane, the governor signed an emergency _____ which sent food and medical aid to the destroyed counties.

Section III: Vocabulary Booster

Fill in the blanks below with the following words to complete the passage.

intended	beneath	wide-spreading	forth	restless
closely	scarcely	certainly	content	attending

No one (1) _____ to leave Martha alone that afternoon, but it happened that everyone was called away, for one reason or another. Mrs. McFarland was (2) _____ the weekly card party. Papa was at the office, as usual. It was Mary Ann's day out. As for Emeline, she (3) _____ should have stayed in the house and looked after the little girl; but Emeline had a (4) _____ nature and felt compelled to be out on such a fine afternoon.

Once, so long ago our great-grandfathers could (5) _____ have heard it mentioned, there lived within the great Forest of Burzee a wood-nymph named Necile. She was (6) _____ related to the mighty Queen Zurline, and her home was (7) _____ the shade of a (8) _____ oak. Once every year, on Budding Day, when the trees put (9) _____ their new buds, it was believed that the Necile would appear and dance to her heart's (10) _____ to celebrate of the budding of the trees.

Section IV: Synonyms Booster

Select one word that has the closest meaning to the word on the left.

1	**Aloof**	Detached	Friendly	Warm	Attached	Serious
2	**Livid**	Assuage	Wrathful	Loved	Joyful	Placid
3	**Deplete**	Thorough	Err	Intend	Develop	Exhaust
4	**Exceptional**	Crushing	Intolerable	Facile	Remarkable	Easy
5	**Onerous**	Burdensome	Horrid	Enjoyable	Warm	Calm

Passage 7

Dantes felt more gratitude for the possession of this piece of iron than he had ever felt for anything. He had noticed, however, that the prisoner on the other side had ceased his labour. All day he toiled on untiringly, and by the evening he had succeeded in extracting ten handfuls of plaster and fragments of stone. When the hour for his jailer's visit arrived, Dantes straightened the handle of the saucepan as well as he could, and placed it in its accustomed place. Having poured out his ration of soup, the turnkey retired. Dantes wished to ascertain whether his neighbour had really ceased to work. He listened—all was silent.

Section I: *From the passage*

Select the best synonym to replace the word in the sentence.

1   Dantes felt more gratitude for the **possession** of this piece of iron than he had ever felt for anything.

   (a) tenure   (b) obtainment   (c) occupancy   (d) procurement

2   He had noticed, however, that the prisoner on the other side had **ceased** his labour.

   (a) continued   (b) completed   (c) desisted   (d) started

3   All day he **toiled** on untiringly, and by the evening he had succeeded in extracting ten handfuls of plaster and fragments of stone.

   (a) slaved   (b) lazed   (c) idled   (d) ventured

4   When the hour for his jailer's visit arrived, Dantes straightened the handle of the saucepan as well as he could, and placed it in its **accustomed** place.

   (a) abnormal   (b) usual   (c) characteristic   (d) unusual

5   Dantes wished to **ascertain** whether his neighbour had really ceased to work.

   (a) verify   (b) disprove   (c) settle   (d) invalidate

Section II: *More from the passage*

Complete the following crossword puzzle to gain a better understanding of the vocabulary in the passage. The answers to the puzzle can all be found in the passage.

A word for...

Across

2. hard work: _____

7. being thankful: _____

8. not speaking or making noise: _____

9. working very hard and never seeming to get weary: _____

Down

1. a broken part of a piece of something: _____

3. to remove something by pulling it out or cutting it out: _____

4. a food allowance for a day: _____

5. to go to sleep: _____

6. to achieve the correct and desired result: _____

8. to put something in order: _____

Section III: Vocabulary Booster

Fill in the blanks below with the following words to complete the passage.

redeem	thrifty	lacklustre	protest	associated
penury	laughingly	reclaim	affluence	transient

Mrs. Mingott had long since succeeded in untying her husband's fortune, and had lived in (1) _____ for half a century; but memories of her early straits had made her excessively (2) _____, and though, when she bought an extravagant dress or a fine piece of furniture from time to time, she could not bring herself to spend much on the (3) _____ pleasures of the table. Therefore, for totally different reasons, her food was as poor, and her wines did nothing to (4) _____ it. Her relatives considered the (5) _____ of her table a discredit to the Mingott name, which had always been (6) _____ with good living; but people continued to come to her dinner parties in spite of the (7) _____ food and flat champagne, and in reply to the (8) _____ of her son who tried to (9) _____ the family's reputation by having the best chef in New York, she used to say (10) _____, "What's the use of two good cooks in one family, now that I've married the girls off and can't eat rich sauces anyway?"

Passage 8

Tom found himself in a noble apartment of the palace and heard the door close behind him. Around him stood those who had come with him. Before him, at a little distance, reclined a very large and very fat man, with a wide, pulpy face, and a stern expression. His large head was very grey; and his whiskers, which he wore only around his face, like a frame, were grey also. His clothing was of rich stuff, but old, and slightly frayed in places. One of his swollen legs had a pillow under it, and was dressed in bandages. There was silence now; and everyone's head was bent in reverence.

Section I: *From the passage*

Select the best synonym to replace the word in the sentence.

1   Tom found himself in a **noble** apartment of the palace and heard the door close behind him.

    (a) servile   (b) unrefined   (c) queenly   (d) imperial

2   Before him, at a little distance, **reclined** a very large and very fat man, with a wide, pulpy face, and a stern expression.

    (a) stood   (b) lounged   (c) sat   (d) sprawled

3   His clothing was of rich stuff, but old, and slightly **frayed** in places.

    (a) sewn   (b) tattered   (c) stitched   (d) fragmented

4   One of his swollen legs had a pillow under it, and was **dressed** in bandages.

    (a) adorned   (b) clad   (c) decorated   (d) uncovered

5   There was silence now; and everyone's head was bent in **reverence**.

    (a) shock   (b) acknowledgement   (c) deference   (d) anger

Section II: More from the Passage -- Opposites Attract

Match each word on the left to with its antonym on the right. The first has been done for you.

(1) close   :   h   (a)   deflated

(2) wide   :   _____   (b)   leave

(3) stern   :   _____   (c)   little

(4) swollen   :   _____   (d)   narrow

(5) reverence   :   _____   (e)   clamour

(6) dreaded   :   _____   (f)   straight

(7) large   :   _____   (g)   disdain

(8) old   :   _____   (h)   ~~open~~

(9) silence   :   _____   (i)   lenient

(10) bent   :   _____   (j)   welcomed

(11) come   :   _____   (k)   new

Section III: Vocabulary Booster

Write an antonym for each of the underlined words from the following sentences.

1   Our failure to recycle is causing great levels of   :
    devastation to the planet.   _____

2   The only reason why Bob struggled with spelling was   :
    because of his **slothfulness**.   _____

3   Periods of **austerity** during an economic depression :
    can cause people to become incredibly unhappy.   _____

4   **Gluttony** is a trait that I personally despise.   :
                                                                      _____

5   Jessie **fervently** believes that clowns are vicious and :
    scary.   _____

6   After sleeping for hours, the cat moved leisurely in a :
    languid motion.   _____

7   The **timorous** witness refuses to testify because of the :
    defendant's reputation for being vengeful.   _____

8
    It is appalling that the factory uses **obsolete** machinery :
    that is a threat to the lives of the workers.   _____

9   While Henry seems **obtuse**, he can be sharp as a tack :
    and hold his ground in an academic debate.   _____

10 A most **affable** man, the candidate has a smile for :
    everyone and is always willing to shake hands with   _____
    voters.

Section IV: Synonyms Booster

Select one word that has the closest meaning to the word on the left.

1	**Peruse**	Dismiss	Discover	Overlook	Neglect	Examine

2	**Nonchalant**	Intrigued	Nervous	Placid	Anxious	Excited

3	**Rustic**	Urban	Modern	Knotty	Complex	Rural

4	**Charm**	Trinket	Treasure	Package	Box	Container

5	**Mariner**	Doctor	Sailor	Lawyer	Architect	Teacher

Passage 9

Rabbit was naturally shy, and being only made of velveteen, some of the more expensive toys snubbed him. The mechanical toys were very superior, and looked down upon everyone else; they were full of modern ideas, and pretended they were real. The Rabbit could not claim to be a model of anything, for he didn't know that real rabbits existed; he thought they were all stuffed with sawdust like himself, and he understood that sawdust was quite out-of-date and should never be mentioned in modern circles. Even Timothy, the jointed wooden lion, who was made by the disabled soldiers, and should have had broader views, put on airs and pretended he was connected with Government. Poor little Rabbit was made to feel himself very insignificant and commonplace, and the only person who was kind to him at all was the Skin Horse.

Section I: *From the passage*

Select the best synonym to replace the word in the sentence.

1 Rabbit was naturally shy, and being only made of velveteen, some of the more expensive toys **snubbed** him.

   (a) ostracised (b) respected (c) welcomed (d) offended

2 The mechanical toys were very **superior**, and looked down upon everyone else…

   (a) unremarkable (b) detestable (c) haughty (d) grand

3 …they were full of **modern** ideas, and pretended they were real.

   (a) antiquated (b) ancient (c) fresh (d) contemporary

4 The Rabbit could not **claim** to be a model of anything, for he didn't know that real rabbits existed.

   (a) assert (b) deny (c) request (d) reply

5 Poor little Rabbit was made to feel himself very **insignificant** and commonplace, and the only person who was kind to him at all was the Skin Horse.

   (a) important (b) substantial (c) unimportant (d) petty

Section II: *More from the passage*

Complete the following word search activity to gain a better understanding of the vocabulary in the passage. Begin by answering the questions with a word that can be found in the passage. Next, search for the word you have identified in the puzzle.

```
D  M  W  C  Q  H  G  D  I  H  U  S  L  Z  U
E  A  E  P  I  Z  O  A  E  I  C  Z  I  X  D
F  Z  T  C  I  D  V  H  J  T  A  I  R  S  V
F  A  S  E  H  D  E  L  B  A  S  I  D  U  Q
U  R  S  N  S  A  R  Y  S  D  E  I  Y  X  G
T  Z  G  T  P  T  N  V  U  K  O  T  X  A  Y
S  M  P  B  K  V  M  I  V  W  U  D  K  E  C
S  P  B  Z  E  Z  E  S  C  U  R  Y  C  O  L
K  Y  C  X  F  B  N  H  P  A  L  Q  N  A  A
P  L  Z  E  U  B  T  Y  J  J  L  N  E  G  S
C  O  M  M  O  N  P  L  A  C  E  R  Z  T  H
A  A  A  T  L  S  D  Y  E  C  S  B  W  S  J
L  X  G  I  E  C  V  K  T  R  Q  E  O  V  P
M  J  U  V  M  K  O  E  D  C  G  E  V  T  O
S  G  N  E  E  Z  D  D  A  U  W  L  R  P  M
```

Identify a word or a phrase in the passage that has the same meaning as the following words. The first letter is provided for you.

1	being an actual thing; not imaginary	:	r_____
2	to be associated with	:	c_____
3	gone out of style or fashion	:	out of d_____
4	undistinguished, uninteresting	:	c_____
5	to be filled	:	s_____
6	to be arrogant	:	put on a_____
7	physically impaired	:	d_____
8	the system by which a state or community is ruled	:	g_____
9	had actual being	:	e_____

10   operated by machinery   :   m_____

Section III: Vocabulary Booster
Fill in the blanks below with the following words to complete the passage.

investigating	inappropriate	counsellor	public	recommended
illegal	privacy	exit	randomly	embarrassing

Tips for staying safe on the Internet:

- Be smart about what you post on the Web. It is a lot more public than it seems. Use (1) _____ settings and don't just (2) _____ accept everyone's friend request. Do a bit of (3) _____to find out more about them first. It's (4) _____that you don't use your real name or give out too much personal information on your social media sites.

- Clean up your profile. Take anything(5) _____, too personal or any photos that show you doing something (6) _____off your page.

- Adults who talk to you about sex online are committing a crime. Report any (7) _____ pictures or messages you receive on your mobile phone or online to an adult you trust. Do not keep quiet about this; notify your parents, guardians, teacher or school (8) _____ immediately.

- Be careful if you decide to meet in person someone you met on the Internet. You may think you know them well from their online profiles, but their profiles might not paint an accurate picture of what they are really like. Tell your parents or someone you trust before you go. Don't go alone, bring a friend. Always meet in a (9) _____place. Make sure you have your mobile phone and an (10) _____ plan.

Passage 10

It was a wonderful kitchen; I had many meals there afterwards and I found it a better place to eat in than the grandest dining-room in the world. It was so cosy and home-like and warm. It was so handy for the food too. You took it right off the fire, hot, and put it on the table and ate it. And you could watch your toast toasting at the fender and see it didn't burn while you drank your soup. Then the fireplace—the biggest fireplace you ever saw—was like a room in itself. You could get right inside it even when the logs were burning and sit on the wide seats either side and roast chestnuts after the meal was over—or listen to the kettle singing, or tell stories, or look at picture-books by the light of the fire. It was a marvellous kitchen. It was like the Doctor, comfortable, sensible, friendly and solid.

Section I: *From the passage*

Select the best synonym to replace the word in the sentence.

1   It was a **wonderful** kitchen…

    (a) unexceptional   (b) disagreeable   (c) amazing   (d) common

2   I had many meals there afterwards and I found it a **better** place to eat in than the grandest dining-room in the world.

    (a) secondary   (b) important   (c) humble   (d) superior

3   It was so **cosy** and home-like and warm.

    (a) sheltered   (b) comfortable   (c) cold   (d) sterile

4   It was so **handy** for the food too.

    (a) convenient   (b) adjacent   (c) awkward   (d) inept

5   It was like the Doctor, comfortable, **sensible**, friendly and solid.

    (a) imbecile   (b) rational   (c) discreet   (d) ignorant

Section II: More from the Passage -- Opposites Attract

Match each word on the left with its antonym on the right. The first has been done for you.

(1)	many	:	b	(a)	cold
(2)	afterwards	:	_____	(b)	~~few~~
(3)	warm	:	_____	(c)	begin
(4)	biggest	:	_____	(d)	ordinary
(5)	wide	:	_____	(e)	unpleasant
(6)	over	:	_____	(f)	hostile
(7)	marvellous	:	_____	(g)	beforehand
(8)	comfortable	:	_____	(h)	untrustworthy
(9)	friendly	:	_____	(i)	cramped
(10)	solid	:	_____	(j)	outside
(11)	inside	:	_____	(k)	tiniest

Section III: Vocabulary Booster

Write an antonym for each of the underlined words from each of the following sentences.

1   Joseph arrived at the school disco wearing an **eccentric** claret-coloured hat.   :   _____

2   "I cannot stand cats!" Penelope **vociferated**.   :   _____

3   In order to annoy Jake, Bob continued to **orbit** around him.   :   _____

4   **Haughtiness** is a characteristic that I do not appreciate, especially when I have to work closely with someone like that.   :   _____

5   The Member of Parliament believed that massive reforms would rejuvenate the archaic education system and **enhance** teaching and learning in the classrooms.   :   _____

6   I apologise for being **tardy** in my response to your questions, but I have been swamped with work recently.   :   _____

7   Although Colin was smaller than his other teammates, his **tenacious** attitude allowed him to accomplish as much as they did.   :   _____

8   At the age of thirteen, Percy was so **credulous** he believed in the tooth fairy.   :

    _____

9   Despite the **plethora** of movies offered by the video store, Julie always rents the same movie over and over again.   :   _____

10 Compared to oak trees, the willow's branches are **pliable**, tending to bend gracefully in a strong wind instead of breaking.   :   _____

Section IV: Synonyms Booster

Select one word that has the closest meaning to the word on the left.

1	**Mingle**	Disjoin	Err	Absorb	Admix	Quaff

2	**Amenity**	Facility	Injury	Pain	Regard	Benefit

3	**Amend**	Fix	Convert	Mitigate	Further	Rule

4	**Dire**	Tranquil	Fortunate	Trivial	Immediate	Dreadful

5	**Frazzled**	Maintained	Fixed	Seedy	Spent	Full

4   The police kicked on the door, expecting to catch the criminal red-handed; however the door flew open to **reveal** an old man in his pajamas, standing at the doorway of his kitchen with a mug of tea in his hands and a look of bewilderment on his face.

   (a)   divulge   (b)   cover   (c)   hide   (d)   **show**

5   The factory has been outfitted with state-of-the-art machinery and is ready to **commence** operations next week.

   (a)   end   (b)   **begin**   (c)   work   (d)   cease

6   As the firemen had protective masks on, they did not have to suffer the **acrid** fumes from the burning chemical plant.

   (a)   intense   (b)   savoury   (c)   unpleasant   (d)   **pungent**

7   The patrons of the bar breathed a sigh of relief when the manager removed the **boorish** drunk, who had been traumatising the waitresses and annoying the other patrons, despite repeated warnings.

   (a)   unattractive   (b)   **churlish** (c)   mannerly   (d)   unkind

8   My father holds a certain disdain for politicians and is very **cynical** of anyone who promises to introduce sweeping reforms once they are voted into office.

   (a)   **distrusting** (b)   optimistic   (c)   trusting   (d)   supportive

9   Just because the new teacher scorned dated education practices and had new ideas about teaching strategies that differed from the peers, her views were considered **heresy** and she was even ostracised by her peers.

   (a)   orthodoxy   (b)   **fallacy**   (c)   blasphemy   (d)   dissent

10   In the aftermath of a recent spike of domestic violence, the MP's speech about the necessity of having policies in place to protect victims of such atrocities was **poignant** and left the audience rather sad, but thoughtful.

   (a)   unemotional   (b)   sentimental   (c)   unaffected   (d)   **moving**

Passage 2

Nelson Mandela is widely regarded as being one of the world's most illustrious figures because of his determination to end the racist apartheid regime of South Africa. He believed that society should treat all people regardless of their ethnic, cultural or religious background equally. Despite being imprisoned for twenty-seven years, he defied belief by becoming South Africa's first black president in 1990. He was commemorated for his achievements and was awarded the Nobel Peace Prize in 1993. His story has inspired millions of people to fight for equality, treat others with respect and stand up in the face of injustice.

Section I: *From the passage*
Select the best synonym to replace the word in the sentence.

1   Nelson Mandela is widely regarded as being one of the world's most ***illustrious*** figures because of his determination to end the racist apartheid regime of South Africa.

    (a) regular   (b) **esteemed**   (c) unknown   (d) insignificant

2   He believed that society should treat all people regardless of their ethnic, cultural or religious background ***equally***.

    (a) appropriately (b) **justly**   (c) proportionately (d) unfairly

3   Despite being imprisoned for twenty-seven years, he ***defied*** belief by becoming South Africa's first black president in 1990.

    (a) mocked   (b) **challenged** (c) encouraged (d) complimented

4   He was ***commemorated*** for his achievements and was awarded the Nobel Peace Prize in 1993.

    (a) **memorialised** (b) denounced (c) overlooked (d) monument

5   His story has ***inspired*** millions of people to fight for equality, treat others with respect and stand up in the face of injustice.

    (a) dissuaded (b) discouraged (c) **emboldened** (d) spurned

Section II: Opposites Attract

Match each word on the left to with its antonym on the right. The first has been done for you.

(1)	widely	: d	(a)	equality
(2)	most	: h	(b)	criticism
(3)	end	: f	(c)	truce
(4)	believed	: e	(d)	~~narrowly~~
(5)	achievement	: g	(e)	disregarded
(6)	imprisoned	: k	(f)	begin
(7)	first	: j	(g)	failures
(8)	awarded	: i	(h)	least
(9)	fight	: c	(i)	refused
(10)	respect	: b	(j)	last
(11)	injustice	: a	(k)	liberated

Section III: Vocabulary Booster

Fill in the blank spaces below with the following words to complete the passage:

visage	single-handedly	treasure	irk	resolved
ascending	undertake	determined	escaped	fled

Meanwhile the Captain of the thieves having (1) **escaped** with his life, (2) **fled** to the forest in hot wrath and sore (3) **irk** of mind; and his senses were scattered and the colour of his (4) **visage** vanished like (5) **ascending** smoke. Then he thought the matter over again and again, and at last he firmly (6) **resolved** that he should take the life of Ali, else he would lose all the (7) **treasure** which his enemy, by knowledge of the magical words, would take away and turn to his own use. Furthermore, he was (8) **determined** that he would (9) **undertake** the business (10) **single-handedly**.

Section IV: Synonyms Booster

Select one word that has the closest meaning to the word on the left.

| 1 | **Depreciate** | Choose | Apex | Select | Decrease | Zenith |

Answer = decrease

| 2 | **Churlish** | Truculent | Angelic | Diplomatic | Stubborn | Independent |

Answer = truculent

| 3 | **Poignant** | Rotund | Polished | Exhausted | Happy | Sad |

Answer = sad

| 4 | **Enthusiasm** | Apex | Wisdom | Insincerity | Politeness | Alacrity |

Answer = alacrity

| 5 | **Compassion** | Animosity | Malice | Pity | Gall | Sickness |

Answer = *pity*

Passage 3

Tigers are widely considered to be one of the most fierce and powerful animals on earth. However, despite their supposed strength, they are in fact one of the world's most vulnerable creatures and face a high risk of extinction. Statistics shows that at the beginning of the 20th century, there were more than 100,000 tigers living in the wild. However, by the end of the 20th century, that number had dwindled to approximately 3,000. The greatest threat to the existence of tigers is homo sapiens. Tigers are hunted, stripped of their skin and killed for their body parts. In some parts of the world, the body parts of tigers are a much-desired commodity because they are believed to contain healing properties.

Section I: *From the passage*

Select the best synonym to replace the word in the sentence.

1   Despite their supposed strength, tigers are in fact one of the world's most **vulnerable** creatures and face a high risk of extinction.

    (a) protected   (b) guarded   (c) unsusceptible   (d) **defenceless**

2   **Statistics** show that at the beginning of the 20th century, there were more than 100,000 tigers living in the wild.

    (a) fabrication   (b) concept   (c) **data**   (d) experience

3   However, by the end of the 20th century, that number had **dwindled** to approximately 3,000.

    (a) increased   (b) **declined**   (c) decayed   (d) prolonged

4   Tigers are hunted, **stripped** of their skin and killed for their body parts.

    (a) **divested**   (b) diverted   (c) deprived   (d) disrobed

5   In some parts of the world, the body parts of tigers are a much-desired **commodity** because they are believed to contain healing properties.

    (a) **product**   (b) produce   (c) phenomenon   (d) gizmo

Section II: *More from the passage*

Complete the following crossword puzzle to gain a better understanding of the vocabulary in the passage. The answers to the puzzle can all be found in the passage.

Another word for...

Across

4	the state of being	:	**existence**
6	curing, to make healthy	:	**healing**
7	pursued and captured	:	**hunted**
8	deemed to be	:	**considered**
9	hazard, danger	:	**risk**

Down

1	close to, roughly	:	**approximately**
2	wild, savage, hostile	:	**fierce**
3	physically strong	:	**powerful**
4	dying out, coming to an end	:	**extinction**
5	peril, trouble	:	**threat**

Section III: *Vocabulary Booster*

Fill in the blanks below with the following words to complete the passage.

helpful	items	dense	tendency	impulse
potentially	extremely	apparently	purchasing	advantageous

Shopping for food can be (1) **extremely** enjoyable. However, before (2) **purchasing** anything, it's (3) **advantageous** to know what you want to buy. One way of doing this is to write a shopping list which contains all of the (4) **items** you want to buy. Shopping lists are (5) **helpful** as they can (6) **potentially** save you time and money. Some people believe that one should never shop on an empty stomach. (7) **Apparently**, research findings show that when shoppers are hungry when they shop for food, they have a (8) **tendency** to act on (9) **impulse** and purchase more calorically (10) **dense** food.

Passage 4

Did you know that on average, we spend approximately one third of our lives (25 years) sleeping? However, most of us can barely recollect what we experience during our sleep. During sleep, our bodies commence a sophisticated cycle of renewal that is imperative in reestablishing our health and well-being. Sleep is divided into two stages: stages one and two. During stage one we begin to drift off and our bodies will involuntarily jerk. Scientists refer to this jerking motion as a hypnic jerk. In the second stage of sleep, our body temperatures drop and our hearts begin to slow down. This is followed by deep sleep where our tissues regrow and our immune system is revivified.

Section I: *From the passage*

Select the best synonym to replace the word in the sentence.

1   However, most of us can barely **recollect** what we experience during our sleep.

   (a)   contrive   (b)   lose   (c)   summon   (d)   **remember**

2   During sleep, our bodies commence a sophisticated cycle of renewal that is **imperative** in reestablishing our health and well-being.

   (a)   **critical**   (b)   discretionary   (c)   inessential   (d)   pressing

3   During stage one we begin to drift off and our bodies will **involuntarily** jerk.

   (a)   cautiously   (b)   **uncontrollably**   (c)   unenthusiastically   (d)   warily

4   Scientists refer to this jerking motion as a hypnic **jerk**.

   (a)   twitch   (b)   **jolt**   (c)   wriggle   (d)   shiver

5   This is followed by deep sleep where our tissues regrow and our immune system is **revivified**.

   (a)   enervated   (b)   gladdened   (c)   comforted   (d)   **rejuvenated**

Section II: *More from the passage*

Identify a word or a phrase in the passage that has the same meaning as the following words. The first letter is provided for you.

1	regeneration	:	**renewal**
2	almost not; scarcely	:	**barely**
3	intricate	:	**sophisticated**
4	split	:	**divided**
5	phases	:	**stages**
6	fall asleep	:	**drift off**
7	a typical amount	:	**average**
8	resistant	:	**immune**
9	encounter	:	**experience**
10	movement	:	**motion**

Section III: Vocabulary Booster

Fill in the blanks below with the following words to complete the passage.

centered	maintained	practised	decay	preserving
subsequently	famed	deliberately	vast	thus

The ancient Egyptian civilization is (1) **famed** for its (2) **vast** pyramids which are more than five thousand years old. Daily life in ancient Egypt was heavily (3) **centered** around religious worship and (4) **subsequently** there were many temples. Ancient Egyptians (5) **maintained** a strong belief in the afterlife and (6) **thus** built pyramids as tombs for the pharaohs.

The ancient Egyptians also (7) **practiced** mummification – the art of (8) **preserving** a body, either human or animal. The Egyptian mummies were made by (9) **deliberately** drying the body. By eliminating moisture, the source of (10) **moisture** is removed. They dried the body by using a salt mixture called natron.

Section IV: Synonyms Booster

Select one word that has the closest meaning to the word on the left.

1	**Resolute**	Freedom	Admire	Determined	Evolve	Answer

Answer = determined

2	**Diminish**	Decrease	View	Orbit	Resolve	Discover

Answer = decrease

3	**Revolve**	Enlighten	Polish	Stand	Orbit	Stumble

Answer = orbit

4	**Alleviate**	Intensify	Identify	Hold	Hamper	Relieve

Answer = relieve

5	**Exasperate**	Condemn	Enrage	Falsify	Coat	Approve

Answer = enrage

Passage 5

The Greeks believed that the home of their omnipotent deity, Zeus, was on the top of Mount Olympus – a high and lofty mountain whose summit, wrapt in clouds and mist, was hidden from mortal view. Here youth never ages, and the passing years leave no traces on its favoured inhabitants. On the cloud-capped summit of Olympus was the palace of Zeus and Hera, of burnished gold, chased silver, and gleaming ivory. Lower down were the homes of the other gods, which, though less commanding in position and size, were similar to that of Zeus' in design and workmanship. Below these were other palaces of silver, ebony, ivory, or burnished brass, where the Demi-gods, resided.

Section I: *From the passage*

Select the best synonym to replace the word in the sentence.

1   The Greeks believed that the home of their **omnipotent** deity, Zeus, was on the top of Mount Olympus.

    (a) impotent   (b) important   (c) colossal   (d) **almighty**

2   Mount Olympus was a high and lofty mountain whose summit, wrapt in clouds and mist, was hidden from **mortal** view.

    (a) fatal   (b) **human**   (c) implacable   (d) tangible

3   Here youth never ages, and the passing years leave no traces on its **favoured** inhabitants.

    (a) **privileged**   (b) unpopular   (c) prejudiced   (d) exempted

4   Lower down were the homes of the other gods, which, though less **commanding** in position and size, were similar to that of Zeus' in design and workmanship.

    (a) compelling   (b) decisive   (c) unassertive   (d) **dominating**

5   Below these were other palaces of silver, ebony, ivory, or burnished brass, where the Demi-gods, **resided**.

    (a) **dwelled**   (b) endured   (c) permeated   (d) bunked

Section II: *More from the passage*

Fill in the blanks with the following words to complete the sentences and to gain a better understanding of the vocabulary featured in the passage.

summit	lofty	youth	inhabitants	workmanship
similar	hidden	passing	burnished	deity

1   Let's meet at the **summit** at 3:30 p.m. so we can ski the last run down the mountain together.

2   "Any explanation that relies on something supernatural, such as a **deity**, is not science!" he declared firmly, trying to douse the superstitious beliefs of his aged mother.

3   It is hard to believe that our strait-laced friend was a passionate political activist in his **youth**.

4   There are no rivers or lakes on the islands of Bermuda, so the **inhabitants** must use rain for water.

5   The struggles of life had taken a toll on her – each **passing** year brought new struggles, new obstacles and a couple of lines to her weather-beaten face.

6   Most warranties cover repair or replacement of defective elements due to faulty **workmanship** or materials and are usually in effect for a period of time.

7   The island is mountainous in the main, with a number of **lofty** upland plains in the east, and volcanic in the west.

8   She had taken extra care in her appearance today and her usually wild and unruly hair gleamed like **burnished** copper.

9   She felt the loss already, a pain **similar** to the loss of her beloved mother so many years ago.

10   He had kept his identity **hidden** for five years now, but he knew deep down that it couldn't last forever and dreaded the day when he would have to reveal his true identity to those he had come to love and respect.

Section III: Vocabulary Booster
Fill in the blanks below with the following words to complete the passage.

casual	whites	job	folded	wedding
formal	laundry	tie	occasions	suit

Different clothes are required for different (1) **occasions**. For (2) **formal** occasions such as a (3) **job** interview or a friend's (4) **wedding**, men might wear a formal (5) **suit** and a (6) **tie**. For informal occasions such as a backyard barbeque, they will probably wear something (7) **casual** such as a pair of jeans and a T-shirt.

When your clothes get dirty, it's time to do the (8) **laundry**. Usually clothes are separated into the (9) **whites** and the colours. After the clothes are washed and dried, they are ironed or (10) **folded** and put away.

Passage 6

They travelled on without speech, saving their breath for the work of their bodies. On every side was the silence, pressing upon them with a tangible presence. It affected their minds as the many atmospheres of deep water affect the body of the diver. It crushed them with the weight of unending vastness and unalterable decree. It crushed them into the remotest recesses of their own minds, pressing out of them, like juices from the grape, all the false ardours and exaltations and undue self-values of the human soul, until they perceived themselves finite and small, specks and motes, moving with weak cunning and little wisdom amidst the play and inter-play of the great blind elements and forces.

Section I: *From the passage*

Select the best synonym to replace the word in the sentence.

1   On every side was the silence, pressing upon them with a **tangible** presence.

    (a)   imperceptible   (b)   abstract   (c)   sensible   (d)   **palpable**

2   It crushed them with the weight of unending vastness and **unalterable** decree.

    (a)   inflexible   (b)   required   (c)   **unchangeable** (d)   unbroken

3   It **crushed** them into the remotest recesses of their own minds…

    (a)   **trampled**   (b)   embraced   (c)   crowded   (d)   surrendered

4   …pressing out of them, like juices from the grape, all the false **ardours** and exaltations and undue self-values of the human soul…

    (a)   apathy   (b)   lethargy   (c)   pretentions (d)   **zeal**

5   …until they perceived themselves **finite** and small, specks and motes, moving with weak cunning and little wisdom amidst the play and inter-play of the great blind elements and forces.

    (a)   endless   (b)   **limited**   (c)   exact   (d)   unfixed

Section II: *More from the passage*

Fill in the blanks with the following words to complete the sentences and to gain a better understanding of the vocabulary featured in the passage.

remotest	exaltation	atmosphere	perceived	presence
decree	vastness	undue	speech	speck

1   The **vastness** of the region has always given its people an independent, frontiersman spirit.

2   The doctor said that he would be able to go home in ten days, provided he wasn't subjected to any **undue** stress.

3   She heaved with painful sobs, rendering **speech** impossible.

4   By the time they made it to the cafeteria, three hours after the designated lunch hour, not a **speck** of food was in sight.

5   She had not seen him for so long that his **presence** was the best part of her birthday party.

6   Of existing species the bear, wild-boar, badger and roe-deer may occasionally be seen in the **remotest** wilds of mountain and forest.

7   Being ever the most consummate host, she firmly believed that having live music could really add to the celebratory **atmosphere** as guests relax and enjoy themselves.

8   She beamed with **exaltation** at the thought of finally being able to marry the love of her life.

9   It is a marketing fact that mediocre products are **perceived** to be more valuable if they are overpriced.

10 After the hurricane, the governor signed an emergency **decree** which sent food and medical aid to the destroyed counties.

Section III: Vocabulary Booster

Fill in the blanks below with the following words to complete the passage.

intended	beneath	wide-spreading	forth	restless
closely	scarcely	certainly	content	attending

No one (1) **intended** to leave Martha alone that afternoon, but it happened that everyone was called away, for one reason or another. Mrs. McFarland was (2) **attending** the weekly card party. Papa was at the office, as usual. It was Mary Ann's day out. As for Emeline, she (3) **certainly** should have stayed in the house and looked after the little girl; but Emeline had a (4) **restless** nature and felt compelled to be out on such a fine afternoon.

Once, so long ago our great-grandfathers could (5) **scarcely** have heard it mentioned, there lived within the great Forest of Burzee a wood-nymph named Necile. She was (6) **closely** related to the mighty Queen Zurline, and her home was (7) **beneath** the shade of a (8) **wide-spreading** oak. Once every year, on Budding Day, when the trees put (9) **forth** their new buds, it was believed that the Necile would appear and dance to her heart's (10) **content** to celebrate of the budding of the trees.

Section IV: Synonyms Booster

Select one word that has the closest meaning to the word on the left.

1	Aloof	Detached	Friendly	Warm	Attached	Serious

Answer = detached

2	Livid	Assuage	Wrathful	Loved	Joyful	Placid

Answer = wrathful

3	Deplete	Thorough	Err	Intend	Develop	Exhaust

Answer = exhaust

4	Exceptional	Crushing	Intolerable	Facile	Remarkable	Easy

Answer = remarkable

| 5 | **Onerous** | Burdensome | Horrid | Enjoyable | Warm | Calm |

Answer = burdensome

Passage 7

Dantes felt more gratitude for the possession of this piece of iron than he had ever felt for anything. He had noticed, however, that the prisoner on the other side had ceased his labour. All day he toiled on untiringly, and by the evening he had succeeded in extracting ten handfuls of plaster and fragments of stone. When the hour for his jailer's visit arrived, Dantes straightened the handle of the saucepan as well as he could, and placed it in its accustomed place. Having poured out his ration of soup, the turnkey retired. Dantes wished to ascertain whether his neighbour had really ceased to work. He listened—all was silent.

Section I: *From the passage*

Select the best synonym to replace the word in the sentence.

1   Dantes felt more gratitude for the **possession** of this piece of iron than he had ever felt for anything.

    (a) tenure   (b) **obtainment** (c) occupancy (d) procurement

2   He had noticed, however, that the prisoner on the other side had **ceased** to labour.

    (a) continued   (b) completed   (c) **desisted**   (d) started

3   All day he **toiled** on untiringly, and by the evening he had succeeded in extracting ten handfuls of plaster and fragments of stone.

    (a) **slaved**   (b) lazed   (c) idled   (d) ventured

4   When the hour for his jailer's visit arrived, Dantes straightened the handle of the saucepan as well as he could, and placed it in its **accustomed** place.

    (a) abnormal   (b) **usual**   (c) characteristic (d) unusual

5   Dantes wished to **ascertain** whether his neighbour had really ceased to work.

    (a) **verify**   (b) disprove   (c) settle   (d) invalidate

Section II: *More from the passage*

Complete the following crossword puzzle to gain a better understanding of the vocabulary in the passage. The answers to the puzzle can all be found in the passage.

A word for...

Across
2. hard work: **labour**
7. being thankful: **gratitude**
8. not speaking or making noise: **silent**
9. working very hard and never seeming to get weary: **untiring**

Down
1. a broken part of a piece of something: **fragment**
3. to remove something by pulling it out or cutting it out: **extract**
4. a food allowance for a day: **ration**
5. to go to sleep: **retire**
6. to achieve the correct and desired result: **succeed**
8. to put something in order: **straighten**

Section III: Vocabulary Booster

Fill in the blanks below with the following words to complete the passage.

redeem	thrifty	lacklustre	protest	associated
penury	laughingly	reclaim	affluence	transient

Mrs. Mingott had long since succeeded in untying her husband's fortune, and had lived in (1) **affluence** for half a century; but memories of her early straits had made her excessively (2) **thrifty** and though, when she bought an extravagant dress or a fine piece of furniture from time to time, she could not bring herself to spend much on the (3) **transient** pleasures of the table. Therefore, for totally different reasons, her food was as poor, and her wines did nothing to (4) **redeem** it. Her relatives considered the (5) **penury** of her table a discredit to the Mingott name, which had always been (6) **associated** with good living; but people continued to come to her dinner parties in spite of the (7) **lacklustre** food and flat champagne, and in reply to the (8) **protest** of her son who tried to (9) **reclaim** the family's reputation by having the best chef in New York, she used to say (10) **laughingly**, "What's the use of two good cooks in one family, now that I've married the girls off and can't eat rich sauces anyway?"

Passage 8

Tom found himself in a noble apartment of the palace and heard the door close behind him. Around him stood those who had come with him. Before him, at a little distance, reclined a very large and very fat man, with a wide, pulpy face, and a stern expression. His large head was very grey; and his whiskers, which he wore only around his face, like a frame, were grey also. His clothing was of rich stuff, but old, and slightly frayed in places. One of his swollen legs had a pillow under it, and was dressed in bandages. There was silence now; and everyone's head was bent in reverence.

Section I: *From the passage*

Select the best synonym to replace the word in the sentence.

1   Tom found himself in a **noble** apartment of the palace and heard the door
     close behind him.

     (a) servile   (b) unrefined   (c) queenly   (d) **imperial**

2   Before him, at a little distance, **reclined** a very large and very fat man,
     with a wide, pulpy face, and a stern expression.

     (a) stood   (b) **lounged**   (c) sat   (d) sprawled

3   His clothing was of rich stuff, but old, and slightly **frayed** in places.

     (a) sewn   (b) **tattered**   (c) stitched   (d) fragmented

4   One of his swollen legs had a pillow under it, and was **dressed** in
     bandages.

     (a) adorned   (b) **clad**   (c) decorated   (d) uncovered

5   There was silence now; and everyone's head was bent in **reverence**.

     (a) shock   (b) acknowledgement (c) **deference** (d) anger

Section II: More from the Passage -- Opposites Attract

Match each word on the left to with its antonym on the right. The first has been done for you.

(1)	close	:	h	(a)	deflated
(2)	wide	:	**d**	(b)	leave
(3)	stern	:	**i**	(c)	little
(4)	swollen	:	**a**	(d)	narrow
(5)	reverence	:	**g**	(e)	clamour
(6)	dreaded	:	**j**	(f)	straight
(7)	large	:	**c**	(g)	disdain
(8)	old	:	**k**	(h)	~~open~~
(9)	silence	:	**e**	(i)	lenient
(10)	bent	:	**f**	(j)	welcomed
(11)	come	:	**b**	(k)	new

Section III: Vocabulary Booster

Write an antonym for each of the underlined words from each of the following sentences.

1	Our failure to recycle is causing great levels of **devastation** to the planet.	:	**construction**
2	The only reason why Bob struggled with spelling was because of his **slothfulness**.	:	**diligence**
3	Periods of **austerity** during an economic depression can cause people to become incredibly unhappy.	:	**extravagance**
4	**Gluttony** is a trait that I personally despise.	:	**restraint**
5	Jessie **fervently** believes that clowns are vicious and scary.	:	**nonchalantly**
6	After sleeping for hours, the cat moved leisurely in a **languid** motion.	:	**energetic**
7	The **timorous** witness refuses to testify because of the defendant's reputation for being vengeful.	:	**forthcoming**
8	It is appalling that the factory uses **obsolete** machinery that is a threat to the lives of the workers.	:	**new**
9	While Henry seems **obtuse**, he is can be sharp as a tack and hold his ground in an academic debate.	:	**intelligent**
10	A most **affable** man, the candidate has a smile for everyone and is always willing to shake hands with voters.	:	**unfriendly**

Section IV: Synonyms Booster

Select one word that has the closest meaning to the word on the left.

1	**Peruse**	Dismiss	Discover	Overlook	Neglect	Examine

Answer = examine

2	**Nonchalant**	Intrigued	Nervous	Placid	Anxious	Excited

Answer = placid

3	**Rustic**	Urban	Modern	Knotty	Complex	Rural

Answer =rural

4	**Charm**	Trinket	Treasure	Package	Box	Container

Answer = trinket

5	**Mariner**	Doctor	Sailor	Lawyer	Architect	Teacher

Answer = sailor

Passage 9

Rabbit was naturally shy, and being only made of velveteen, some of the more expensive toys snubbed him. The mechanical toys were very superior, and looked down upon everyone else; they were full of modern ideas, and pretended they were real. The Rabbit could not claim to be a model of anything, for he didn't know that real rabbits existed; he thought they were all stuffed with sawdust like himself, and he understood that sawdust was quite out-of-date and should never be mentioned in modern circles. Even Timothy, the jointed wooden lion, who was made by the disabled soldiers, and should have had broader views, put on airs and pretended he was connected with Government. Poor little Rabbit was made to feel himself very insignificant and commonplace, and the only person who was kind to him at all was the Skin Horse.

Section I: *From the passage*

Select the best synonym to replace the word in the sentence.

1   Rabbit was naturally shy, and being only made of velveteen, some of the more expensive toys **snubbed** him.

    (a) **ostracised** (b) respected   (c) welcomed   (d) offended

2   The mechanical toys were very **superior**, and looked down upon everyone else…

    (a) unremarkable (b) detestable (c) **haughty**   (d) grand

3   …they were full of **modern** ideas, and pretended they were real.

    (a) antiquated (b) ancient   (c) fresh   (d) **contemporary**

4   The Rabbit could not **claim** to be a model of anything, for he didn't know that real rabbits existed.

    (a) **assert**   (b) deny   (c) request   (d) reply

5   Poor little Rabbit was made to feel himself very **insignificant** and commonplace, and the only person who was kind to him at all was the Skin Horse.

    (a) important (b) substantial (c) **unimportant** (d) petty

Section II: *More from the passage*

Identify a word or a phrase in the passage that has the same meaning as the following words.
The first letter is provided for you.

1   being an actual thing; not imaginary   :   **real**
2   to be associated with   :   **connected**
3   gone out of style or fashion   :   **out of date**
4   undistinguished, uninteresting   :   **commonplace**
5   to be filled   :   **stuffed**
6   to be arrogant   :   **put on airs**
7   physically impaired   :   **disabled**
8   the system by which a state or community is :   **government**
    ruled
9   had actual being   :   **existed**
10 operated by machinery   :   **mechanical**

Section III: Vocabulary Booster

Fill in the blanks below with the following words to complete the passage.

investigating	inappropriate	counsellor	public	recommended
illegal	privacy	exit	randomly	embarrassing

Tips for staying safe on the Internet:

- Be smart about what you post on the Web. It is a lot more public than it seems. Use (1) **privacy** settings and don't just (2) **randomly** accept everyone's friend request. Do a bit of (3) **investigating** to find out more about them first. It's (4) **recommended** that you don't use your real name or give out too much personal information on your social media sites.

- Clean up your profile. Take anything(5) **embarrassing**, too personal or any photos that show you doing something (6) **illegal** off your page.

- Adults who talk to you about sex online are committing a crime. Report any (7) **inappropriate** pictures or messages you receive on your mobile phone or online to an adult you trust. Do not keep quiet about this; notify your parents, guardians, teacher or school (8) **counsellor** immediately.

- Be careful if you decide to meet in person someone you met on the Internet. You may think you know them well from their online profiles, but their profiles might not paint an accurate picture of what they are really like. Tell your parents or someone you trust before you go. Don't go alone, bring a friend. Always meet in a (9) **public** place. Make sure you have your mobile phone and an (10) **exit** plan.

Passage 10

It was a wonderful kitchen; I had many meals there afterwards and I found it a better place to eat in than the grandest dining-room in the world. It was so cosy and home-like and warm. It was so handy for the food too. You took it right off the fire, hot, and put it on the table and ate it. And you could watch your toast toasting at the fender and see it didn't burn while you drank your soup. Then the fireplace—the biggest fireplace you ever saw—was like a room in itself. You could get right inside it even when the logs were burning and sit on the wide seats either side and roast chestnuts after the meal was over—or listen to the kettle singing, or tell stories, or look at picture-books by the light of the fire. It was a marvellous kitchen. It was like the Doctor, comfortable, sensible, friendly and solid.

Section I: *From the passage*

Select the best synonym to replace the word in the sentence.

1   It was a **wonderful** kitchen…

   (a) unexceptional (b) disagreeable (c) **amazing** (d) common

2   I had many meals there afterwards and I found it a **better** place to eat in than the grandest dining-room in the world.

   (a) secondary   (b) important   (c) humble   (d) **superior**

3   It was so **cosy** and home-like and warm.

   (a) sheltered   (b) **comfortable** (c) cold   (d) sterile

4   It was so **handy** for the food too.

   (a) **convenient** (b) adjacent   (c) awkward   (d) inept

5   It was like the Doctor, comfortable, **sensible**, friendly and solid.

   (a) imbecile   (b) **rational**   (c) discreet   (d) ignorant

Section II: More from the Passage -- Opposites Attract

Match each word on the left with its antonym on the right. The first has been done for you.

(1)	many	:	b	(a)	cold
(2)	afterwards	:	g	(b)	~~few~~
(3)	warm	:	a	(c)	begin
(4)	biggest	:	k	(d)	ordinary
(5)	wide	:	i	(e)	unpleasant
(6)	over	:	c	(f)	hostile
(7)	marvellous	:	d	(g)	beforehand
(8)	comfortable	:	e	(h)	untrustworthy
(9)	friendly	:	f	(i)	cramped
(10)	solid	:	h	(j)	outside
(11)	inside	:	j	(k)	tiniest

Section III: Vocabulary Booster

Write an antonym for each of the underlined words from each of the following sentences.

1   Joseph arrived at the school disco wearing an   :   **conventional**
    eccentric claret-coloured hat.

2   "I cannot stand cats!" Penelope **vociferated**.   :   **concealed**

3   In order to annoy Jake, Bob continued to **orbit** around   :   **shun**
    him.

4   **Haughtiness** is a characteristic that I do not   :   **humility**
    appreciate, especially when I have to work closely with
    someone like that.

5   The Member of Parliament believed that massive   :   **undermine**
    reforms would rejuvenate the archaic education system
    and **enhance** teaching and learning in the classrooms.

6   I apologise for being **tardy** in my response to your   :   **prompt**
    questions, but I have been swamped with work
    recently.

7   Although Colin was smaller than his other teammates,   :   **irresolute**
    his **tenacious** attitude allowed him to accomplish as
    much as they did.

8   At the age of thirteen, Percy was so **credulous** he   :   **sceptical**
    believed in the tooth fairy.

9   Despite the **plethora** of movies offered by the video   :   **scarcity**
    store, Julie always rents the same movie over and over
    again.

10 Compared to oak trees, the willow's branches are   :   **inflexible**
    pliable, tending to bend gracefully in a strong wind
    instead of breaking.

Section IV: Synonyms Booster

Select one word that has the closest meaning to the word on the left.

| 1 | **Mingle** | Disjoin | Err | Absorb | Admix | Quaff |

Answer = Admix

| 2 | **Amenity** | Facility | Injury | Pain | Regard | Benefit |

Answer = Facility

| 3 | **Amend** | Fix | Convert | Mitigate | Further | Rule |

Answer = Fix

| 4 | **Dire** | Tranquil | Fortunate | Trivial | Immediate | Dreadful |

Answer = dreadful

| 5 | **Frazzled** | Maintained | Fixed | Seedy | Spent | Full |

Answer = spent

About The Author

Since 2010, The Tutoress (founded by Victoria Olubi) and her team of dedicated tutors have helped hundreds of children to pass the SATs and 11+ school entrance exams.

As a result of such committed efforts, The Tutoress has maintained an incredible success rate (100% in 2014) and has quickly risen to become one of the leading providers of 11+ tuition in the UK.

Miss Olubi and her team hold fun yet highly effective holiday classes, workshops and intensive courses for students who want to excel in the 11+ exams and beyond.

For more information and for access to free education resources visit www.thetutoress.com.

The Clever Comprehension Academy

Would you love to see your child improve their reading comprehension, grammar, spelling and punctuation skills?

If so, take a look at our brand new online tutoring programme which enables children to study all of the core English Literacy topics without having to leave the house.

The course is **National Curriculum aligned** and features worksheets, online tutorial videos and audios that your child can access 24/7. It's also incredibly affordable. Visit **TheTutoress.com** to sign up.

CPSIA information can be obtained at www.ICGtesting.com
Printed in the USA
LVOW09s1623010416

481786LV00024B/662/P